Going on a Promise

Stories of Abraham

by Aiden Schlichting Enns and Jeremy Bergen

Genesis is a bargain. It contains two stories for the price of one. The first is sometimes called the "prehistory," encompassing the first eleven chapters of Genesis. It is the story of creation and re-creation, followed by a second story (Gen. 12—50), the story of God's chosen people, whom we think of as our ancestors in the faith.

There are many parallels between the two main sections of Genesis, the primary one being that they are both stories of beginnings. Where the first is the story of the beginning of the world, the second is the story of the beginning of faith. Both create something out of nothing. God created the world from a void. And God created a people of faith from a barren couple. Both report God's blessing to the world, the blessing of relating to the people personally. In the first story, God creates people to be companions to each other and to God. In the second story, God creates *a* people to whom to relate. And in both, God gives a promise. At first the promise is that, because of their disobedience, people will suffer hard work and pain in childbirth. But the promise to Abraham is just the opposite. Even to the weak-willed and imperfect people, God promises Abraham both a land of his own and heirs.

> "Deep within us all there is an amazing inner sanctuary of the soul, a holy place, a Divine Center, a speaking Voice, to which we may continuously return. Eternity is at our hearts. . ."
>
> —Thomas R. Kelly, *A Testament of Devotion*

This promise to Abraham sets the whole world on end. It's a promise contingent not on good behavior, but on belief and righteousness. God remembered Noah because he was an exemplary world citizen. He was a good man. God remembers Abraham because he believes. Like the old gospel song that says "I'm going on the promise of his love," there is nothing else on which to base faith.

Genesis 12 is the real beginning of the good news. It is the good news that God loves us beyond belief and in spite of everything, so much so that God can take nothing and make it into something. God can take the unworthy and make us worthy. God can take the weaker and the lesser and make us into the stronger and the greater. That's good news for us.

We struggle, however, with the stories of Abraham. Which one of us could pull up stakes and move today at God's command? Which one of us would willingly offer up a child for sacrifice to demonstrate our own piety? Which one of us wants to risk arguing with God when we barely feel worthy of God's grace sometimes? God invites us into faith freely, but as Abraham can show, believing is costly at times.

Read on to find out for yourself what the cost of faith is…and weigh it against the high price of not believing.

> "Superficiality is the curse of our age. The doctrine of instant satisfaction is a primary spiritual problem. The desperate need today is not for a greater number of intelligent people, or gifted people, but for deep people."
>
> —Richard Foster, *Celebration of Discipline*

About the Writers

Aiden Schlichting Enns is the conference editor for *Canadian Mennonite* and director of communications and publications for the Conference of Mennonites in Canada.

Jeremy Bergen is the coordinator of peace and justice ministries for the Conference of Mennonites in Canada. Both men live in Winnipeg, Manitoba.

Welcome to Good Ground!

Now that you know a little about the topic for this unit, let us introduce you to Good Ground, the series. Good Ground is a unique approach to Bible study. It lets the Bible ask most of the questions and lets participants struggle with the answers. When we ask, "How can I be saved?" the Bible asks, "Whom will you serve?" When we ask, "What will happen to me when I die?" the Bible asks, "What does the Lord require of you?" When we ask, "Whom does God love best?" the Bible asks, "Who is your neighbor?" Good Ground goes to the Scriptures for questions, not just answers.

Here's how each session is structured and what you can expect:

PART I: PREPARATION

We assume that you want to dig into Bible texts enough to do a little reading and thinking between sessions. In this section you are given the Bible passage(s) for the session, a key verse, a summary of the text and the issues it raises, and a three-page study on the text. The section concludes with "Things to think about," which offers some practical applications for everyday living.

We realize that in an age of prepackaged goods and 15-second sound bytes, advance preparation may be a challenge. At the same time, we believe that for God's Word to be relevant to us, we need to do what it takes to ready our hearts and minds.

PART II: SESSION

Here we offer tips for your group when it meets, whether at church, in a home, or in some other setting. Good Ground uses a method for study that begins with everyday life (Focus), moves into an examination of what the Bible says (Engage the Text), then suggests life applications (Respond). The Closing wraps up the study in a brief worship experience.

One of the unique features about Good Ground studies is that they tap into a variety of learning styles. Some people learn best through the traditional lecture and discussion, but many others learn through visuals, imagination, poetry, role-playing and the like. Through these varied learning experiences, Good Ground gets participants involved in the learning, moving beyond the head and into concrete living from the heart.

PART III: LEADER GUIDELINES

We recognize that in many adult groups today, responsibility for leading is passed around within the group—hence the inclusion of notes for the leader in the participant's book. For these sessions to work best, however, those who lead must be prepared ahead of time. This section outlines what materials will be needed for the session, suggests some resources, and offers some tips for making the session come alive. If you are a regular leader of Good Ground, you will likely be aware of our other teaching/leading resources that orient you to our learning philosophy and methods.

Enjoy working with Good Ground as you journey in your faith, growing to be more like Christ!

Julie Garber, editor
Byron Rempel-Burkholder, editor
Ken Hawkley, adult education consultant

Session 1
The Promise of a Blessing

PART I: PREPARATION

Bible passage: Genesis 12:1-8

Key verse: In you all the families of the earth shall be blessed (Gen. 12:3b).

Summary: In the first eleven chapters of Genesis, God is filling the world, scattering people "over the face of all the earth" (Gen. 11:9). In chapter 12, God begins to gather in a family. In particular God calls Abram and promises to make his family a great nation and a blessing to others. How will this man and his barren wife become a great nation and the channel of all blessings? For that matter, how are we, with all our shortcomings, a blessing to others?

Study: In the Bible God regularly "scatters" people. It's the way the word of God gets carried to all corners of the world. Already in Genesis God has populated the earth once, destroyed it, and started over with Noah, scattering his family and pairs of all the species into the world. Then just before Abraham is introduced, God scatters the people who built the Tower of Babel. They stubbornly tried to stick together, but God needed them to go out, so God confounded their language and made it impossible for them to talk to each other.

At first Abraham is called Abram and Sarah is called Sarai. Abram and Abraham are often used interchangeably. Abram (which probably means "the father is exalted") received the new name Abraham (which means "father of multitudes") after he received the promise of God's covenant and future progeny (Gen. 17). Sarai and Sarah are also used interchangeably. The difference between these two names is not clear. They both probably mean "princess" or "mistress." Sarai's name changed to Sarah when God blessed her saying "she shall give rise to nations."

—Genesis 17:16

They had to go out and become the peoples that populated the far reaches of the earth. The story of Abraham and Sarah is also a story of creating a people and sending them out into the world to be a blessing.

The first eleven chapters of the Bible are sometimes called the "prehistory." They tell of God's created order, out of which the story of the people of God arises. Then chapter 12 begins the story of God and God's people. Note some of the parallels and contrasts in the opening of Genesis and the beginning of the Abraham story. In both, God is creating and filling the earth. Genesis 1 and 2 tell how the entire world is made from nothing but chaos and filled with plants and creatures. In Genesis 12, God promises to create a nation from Abraham who is 75 years old and has no children. God is again creating something from nothing. Then God places Adam and Eve in a garden; and God sends Abraham to Canaan, described in Exodus as "the land flowing with milk and honey." In another parallel, both Adam and Eve and Abraham and Sarah commit a deception. The first couple eats of the fruit and lies about it. In Genesis 12:10-20, Abraham and Sarah lie about their relationship as husband and wife to save themselves.

The great difference in these stories, however, is that, for Adam and Eve's deception, God condemns humanity to hard labor, pain in childbirth, and life in an inhospitable earth, but Abraham and Sarah are about to receive a blessing that reverses the curses on Adam and Eve. Though they are well past childbearing years, they will have children and become a great nation. They will also have land, land that is so bountiful the living will be comparatively easy. This is God's blessing for the world.

What We Know

It is difficult to determine the historical timing of Abraham and Sarah. Scholars offer dates anywhere from 2000 B.C. to 1200 B.C. as possible time frames. Many say the stories in Genesis 12 were written down at a significantly later time, perhaps during the time of King David or even later. As a result, facts about the culture during the time of Abraham are difficult to determine.

It is likely that Ur, the place of Abraham's origin, and Haran, the city from which God called him to Canaan, were both relatively well-established commercial and cultural urban centres. This is in contrast to Canaan, which was less developed and inhabited by both nomads and permanent residents.

Socially, the Ancient Near East was organized into patriarchal households where the "father" made the decisions. Abraham moved from place to place with a contingent that included his wife, servants, slaves, and livestock. In Genesis 14:14 he was able to raise an army of 318 from his household alone.

Other Gods

The religious context of the time was polytheism. Abraham's ancestors likely worshiped other gods, perhaps the gods of the moon, which were the gods of Ur. In Canaan, the chief god was El, and people often related to the chief god through lesser, intermediary gods. In any case, the idea of a human being establishing a personal relationship with a god was well known in the time of Abraham. The unique feature of Abraham's God, however, is that God initiated the personal relationship. Abraham made no sacrifices nor prayed any prayers to God to earn God's good grace. Rather, God came to Abraham with a blessing.

> Blessing has been most frequently understood in terms of benefits conveyed—prosperity, power, and especially fertility. This focus on the content of the benefit is now being viewed as secondary. The primary factor of blessing is the statement of relationship between parties.
>
> —from *The Anchor Bible Dictionary*

Promise of Blessing

From seemingly nowhere, God comes to Abraham and promises a blessing. What is a blessing? Is it wealth? good health? happiness? many children? Is it favor that God bestows without reason? The modern mind probably puts little stock in these kinds of blessing. Most of us leave little to fortune or providence and rely on earning the things we have. So what does blessing mean?

To Abraham, a blessing from God conveys not just a thing, but a certain reality. It is God's promise of life in the fullest sense. To most of us, "life" implies physical health and well-being, security, prosperity, and fertility. However, these benefits of blessing are secondary. Primarily, a blessing denotes a particular relationship between parties. God is offering Abraham a relationship with all its accompanying benefits—descendants, land, and whatever else the blessing will bring.

Abraham is blessed because of his relationship with God. It's remarkable that this couple, whose clan undoubtedly worshiped the local gods, responds with faith and obedience to God's call, moving to a new land with only the promise of God as security. In turn, it will be through this type of relationship Abraham has with God that the other families of the earth will be blessed. They too can come into relationship with God and enjoy life to the fullest. Genesis scholar Walter Brueggemann points out in his commentary that Abraham moves into Canaan not to conquer it for God or do anything, really. He is sent to live among the Canaanites, letting the blessing do its work through him.

In the Old Testament, Abraham and Sarah are the parents of the people of God, a people set apart from other nations. In the New Testament, all of humanity is invited into the community of God—a universal invitation that is hinted at in the promise to Abraham. "I will bless you, and make your name great, so that you will be a blessing. I will bless those who bless you, and the one who curses you I will curse; and in you all the families of the earth shall be blessed" (Gen. 12:2-3). Can we, like Abraham, accept the offer of God's relationship and all that it means with a firm yes, leave all that we know, and go to be a blessing to the world? A young man asked Jesus the same question (Matt. 19:20-21). How will we answer it for ourselves?

> Blessed are the peacemakers, for they will be called children of God.
>
> —Matthew 5:9

Things to think about: Talk to three or four people this week about their relationship with God. Think about your own relationship with God. How are you and the people you know blessed? How are you a blessing to others?

PART II: SESSION

Focus (10 MINUTES)

Mingle and visit for the first ten minutes of the session. As you're talking and sharing, write on posted sheets some of the blessings you know—Irish blessings, meal blessings, birthday blessings, house blessings (Bless this Mess!), or other common expressions of blessing. Sit in a circle and look over the list of blessings as a group. From this list, what would you say a blessing is?

Transition: God promises Abraham a blessing of descendants and land. But it's not just Abraham's lucky day. God is offering something that is risky and tough.

Engage the Text (30 MINUTES)

Listen as a guest who has been in leadership or mission work tells about his or her work. Then ask the following questions based on Genesis 12:1-8. Introduce each question by reading the biblical verse from which it comes.

Verse 1: How did you hear God's call? What was your reaction? Where in the world do you think God wants us to go today?

Verse 2: Who has been a blessing to you? How? Judging from Abraham's experience, how are we as individuals to be a blessing to others?

Verse 3. What assurances, if any, do you believe God offers those who go out faithfully in God's name?

Verse 4: At what age should missionaries and leaders in the church step back and let younger people take the lead?

Verse 5: How were you able to move an entire family and household to a strange place?

Verse 6: God promised Abraham a land that was already inhabited by Canaanites. Who inhabited the place you worked as a missionary? What right or authority do Christians have to missionize territories where people of another faith live?

Verse 7: What results of your work have you seen? What results do you hope your children will see, even if you don't?

Respond (10 MINUTES)

Reflect on your guest's presentation and the definition of blessing the group made at the beginning of the session. Talk together briefly about how your ideas of blessing may have changed in the course of the session. Then pair up with the person in the group whose birthday is closest to yours, and covenant together to be a blessing to someone in the coming week. Agree to do something together or separately. If separately, check in with each other by phone near the end of the week to find out what the other has done.

Closing (3 MINUTES)

Stand together in a circle. In a time of silent prayer, volunteer a sentence prayer if you wish, saying how this group has been a blessing to you personally.

PART III: LEADER GUIDELINES

Items Needed

Bibles
Chalkboard and chalk or newsprint and markers
Paper and pens

Resources

Brueggemann, Walter. *Genesis* (Interpretation: A Bible Commentary for Teaching and Preaching). Atlanta: John Knox Press, 1982.

Moyers, Bill. *Genesis: A Living Conversation*. New York: Doubleday, 1996.

Tips for Leading

1. As facilitator, there are a few things you can do to increase your chances that every session will be a huge success (however you define success!):

   a. Keep your spirit open to the guidance of God in your midst (God works in mysterious ways).

   b. Find ways to make the topic relevant for at least one person in the group—you! The session will have a far greater impact on the group if you as a facilitator are genuinely experiencing growth through it.

   c. Feel free to adapt the activities in the session to the needs of the group.

   d. Pay careful attention to what people in the group are saying and doing. As you notice important things that people say, ask them (or others) to expand, explain, or give an example.

2. Introduce visitors and newcomers in this and every session.

3. Invite a former missionary or church leader to visit and be interviewed by the group. Provide the questions in Engage the Text to the guest so he or she can reflect on responses ahead of time. Be prepared to moderate the interview, but open the discussion to the entire group after the guest has had a chance to respond.

4. To prepare for the Focus, write the first few blessings on the posted sheets to get others thinking. As soon as people arrive, invite them to write blessings on the posted sheets. Don't wait until everyone has gathered before starting.

5. Draw quiet people into discussion by asking for their opinions or experience. Encourage frequent contributors to the discussion to hold additional comments until everyone has had a chance to speak. If necessary, give people a time limit for speeches and keep to it rigorously.

Looking ahead: Collect items needed for the voting exercise in Focus in Session 2. If you choose to make bumper stickers in Respond, gather materials for that exercise too.

Session 2
I Believe You Anyway ◼

PART I: PREPARATION

Bible passage: Genesis 15:1-6

Key verse: And he believed the LORD; and the LORD reckoned it to him as righteousness (Gen. 15:6).

Summary: The Lord promises Abraham many descendants. Yet Abraham and his wife Sarah are both old and past childbearing years. It seems impossible that God would give them even one child, let alone enough to fill a galaxy. In spite of this, Abraham believes God and is therefore considered righteous. Abraham believes before the results are in. Is his faith blind? Is it naive? Is it a faith born of hope (there is nowhere but up from here)? To what kind of faith does God call us?

> God promises heirs to Abraham and Sarah, but Abraham is 100 years old and Sarah 90. "It had ceased to be with Sarah after the manner of women" (18:11). The couple's response to the news that Sarah would have a baby is to laugh. When the baby is born, he is named "Isaac," the Hebrew word for laugh.

Study: At first glance Genesis 15:1-6 appears to be about the promise of descendants and land. After all, if Abraham is to have many descendants, he will need the land on which they will live. But on closer examination, this passage is more about faith. God offers a promise, Abraham questions the possibility, God reiterates the offer, whereupon Abraham believes. There are no assurances or guarantees. In fact, the opposite is true. All the evidence could have led Abraham to doubt, but instead he believes, and because of his faith he is considered "righteous."

Finding a Son

Before God promised descendants, we learn in verse 2 that Abram had apparently adopted Eliezer of Damascus, a slave in his household, to be his heir. This was accepted practice for fathers without natural sons in that culture. But why would this already elderly couple have adopted a son at this late date? Because the son can care for the parents in old age, ensure their proper burial and mourning, and receive the inheritance. Adoption was only a stopgap measure, however. If the first wife were to finally bear a son, the child of this primary marriage union would automatically precede the adopted one.

Besides adopting a son, Abraham and Sarah had other options. As we see in Genesis 16, Abraham produced an heir through Sarah's slave, Hagar. Concubinage (marrying a second or more wives) was also an acceptable mechanism by which to produce an heir in Abraham's culture. But hadn't God promised a child to Sarah? Abraham looks at himself and sees that he and Sarah are too old to have children. He naturally questions God's promise. He's not naive and resists the temptations of a naive faith.

In ancient Israelite culture, concubines were slaves in Hebrew households, purchased from poor families, taken in payment of a debt, or captured in war. As wives of lesser ranking, concubines often produced heirs for the head of the household and benefitted from lesser family rights and privileges, such as having their own quarters, food, and clothing. Children born to concubines and the husband were often co-heirs, if not full heirs. While the scripture promotes monogamy, many instances of polygamy and concubinage appear in the Old Testament. Concubinage was a fact of life for powerful agricultural and nomadic families that relied on heirs to carry on the work.

Dialogue with God

Abraham seems bold as he confesses his doubts to God. He doesn't seem to fear that God will strike him down for saying "You have given me no offspring." Honest dialogue with God appears numerous times in the biblical tradition. Job speaks honestly to God about what is right (Job 42:7); the psalmist reminds God of God's promises (Ps.74); even Jesus cries out in anguish on the cross (Mark 15:34).

Bible scholar Gerald Janzen notes in his commentary on Genesis 12–50 that to challenge God requires trust. Even as doubts about the promise creep into Abram's mind, he trusts that questioning God will not be the end of their relationship (Janzen 36). God has already come to him with assurances, saying, "Do not be afraid." In fact, God is pictured here as a shield, not a threatening weapon. So God gives Abraham an opening to lament, and then when Abraham does express his doubts, God repeats the promise of heirs as innumerable as stars (v. 5).

Verse 6 is the climax of the exchange. Will Abraham go along willingly with the plan? Abram "believes," though "trust" perhaps more actively describes his response. There is some relief that Abraham takes the plunge. We don't know what would have happened if he had not. We do know, however, that for his response "the Lord reckoned it to him [Abram] as righteousness" (15:6). In the NIV, the passage is rendered "he credited it to him as righteousness." The Hebrew text contains the possibility of reading it as "he [Abram] credited it to him [God] as righteousness." However we interpret it, it's a good thing.

> Amazing Grace! How sweet the sound,
> that saved a wretch like me!
> I once was lost, but now am found,
> was blind, but now I see.
>
> —John Newton

Intentional Ambiguity

The ambiguity about righteousness may be intentional. We cannot tell who is particularly righteous, God or Abraham, because righteousness describes the actions of both parties in a relationship. Things are right between them.

The Hebrew word for righteousness, *tsedaqah,* was used at times in worship. If a worshiper made a sacrifice acceptable to God, the priest would declare him or her *tsedaqah,* that is, righteous. If a legal action sets things right between people, *tsedaqah* means "justice." If little is turned into much, *tsedaqah* is "prosperity." If fertility results from barrenness, *tsedaqah* means "posterity" (Janzen 38). In each case, things are made right between parties. In Genesis 15, Abraham's share of the transaction between God and him is faith; it is not a rite, a sacrifice, or a proper word. And God's share of the transaction is faith (God will fulfill the promise), and so Abraham considers God to be "righteous."

In a real sense Abraham's faith is blind. Faith by its very definition is blind. "We walk by faith and not by sight" (2 Cor. 5:7). There is much about God we believe without seeing. But while Abraham's faith is blind, it is anything but naive. He has no pie-in-the-sky illusions that the future will be perfect. He is certainly not going on a promise that he will preside over a great nation, but only that his descendants will become a great nation long after him. None of these things convince Abraham to believe. The compelling angle of this story is the right relationship Abraham has with God. It is a relationship of give and take, strong enough to endure doubt, frustration, and delayed gratification. But primarily, Abraham recognizes that faith is a relationship and not just a ritual duty. Relationship is all the reward he needs.

Things to think about: Make a mental list of the people you encountered today and each day this week. In which of these people do you put your faith and trust? What connection, if any, is there between the depth of your relationship with these people and the level of trust you have in each other? Think of your relationship with God in the same way. Where do you come out?

PART II: SESSION

Focus (15 MINUTES)

Sit in a circle. Take a supply of beans (an equal number of two colors or types) from a sack being passed around the circle. As the beans are coming around, think of an exciting story about yourself that you can tell to the group. It can be true or made up. The idea is to confuse others about what is true and what is not. All stories should be plausible. Then take turns telling stories, going alphabetically according to your mother's first name. If you are able, stand to tell your story.

After each story, pass an empty bag around the circle. When it comes to you, vote whether you think the story is true or false, dropping one kind of bean in the bag for "true" or the other kind of bean for "false." After everyone in the group has voted on a story, empty the sack and count the coloured beans. Announce the results to the group. Go on to the next story. Don't discuss whether the story is actually true or not at this point. When all stories have been told and voted on, reveal whether stories were true or false.

> I never spoke with God
> Nor visited in Heaven—
> Yet certain am I of the spot
> As if the Checks were given—
>
> —Emily Dickinson

Transition: How do you know what to believe when someone tells you something, especially when it seems incredible? Abraham had to wrestle with this question when God told him he'd have many descendants. In spite of his old age, Abraham chose to believe God. Let's take a closer look at the story.

Engage the Text (15 MINUTES)

Read Genesis 15:1-6 aloud in parts, one person being the narrator, one reading God's part, and one reading Abraham's lines. If you were to write about Abram's faith today, what would you say? What was unique about his faith in God? What was noble, or worthy of emulating?

At several points in the New Testament, Bible characters reflect on the faith of Abraham. Divide the group into three groups and discuss one of

the following New Testament passages: Romans 4:16-25; Galatians 3:6-14; Hebrews 11:1-3, 8-12.
First read the passage for yourself (or, if the number of Bibles is few, read the passage out loud). Talk about the following questions:

- What does the author think is most important about the story of Abraham and Sarah?
- What happened as a result of Abraham's belief?
- Is there a difference between faith and belief?
- New Testament writers don't refer to Abraham's dialogue with God. What, if any, difference does that make?
- What other differences do you notice between the New Testament accounts of Abraham's righteousness and the Genesis account?

Return to the large group and report briefly on the small group discussion.

Respond (10 MINUTES)

Option A: Abraham discovered that questioning God would not destroy his relationship with God. Take turns telling about a time you questioned God or confronted someone in whom you have faith, such as political leaders, employers, or teachers. Include in your story how you felt when you had to question or confront a person you respect. Also tell how you felt afterward and what happened to your relationship with God or the person.

If you don't have a story to tell, consider telling the group the honest questions you would like to ask of God or the honest questions you would like to ask of people in whom you have faith or trust.

Option B: Make bumper stickers. A popular bumper sticker says "Question Authority." What brief message would Abraham put on a bumper sticker about his relationship with God? If you want to use the slogan as a real bumper sticker, print it on plain self-adhering shelf paper with permanent markers.

Closing (3 MINUTES)

Take time for silent prayer. Reflect for a minute on the marks of a right relationship: good communication, openness, and trust. Then think for another minute on whether or not your relationship with God is right, or could be more right. Ask God to help you become more "righteous." Close by singing or reading the words to "We walk by faith, and not by sight."

PART III: LEADER GUIDELINES

Items Needed

Bibles

Two sacks and a large quantity of dry beans in two different colours (or similar small things such as macaroni and kernels of corn).

Markers and self-adhering shelf paper, cut into strips.

Resources

Janzen, J. Gerald. *Abraham and All the Families of the Earth: A Commentary on the Book of Genesis 12–50*. Grand Rapids: Eerdmans, 1993.

Tips for Leading

1. Read through the entire session. Be prepared to lead out with stories of your own in Focus and Respond. Your experiences may trigger the memories of others.
2. If your group is large, choose several people to tell stories in Focus. Involve everyone in the voting process.
3. Round up items needed for the session, including beans, small paper sacks, markers, and shelf paper.

Looking ahead: Decide now if you would like readers to rehearse the Reader's Theatre in Session 3. Get the group together before the next session to practice their parts. Also, have yarn or ribbon on hand for Respond in Session 3.

Session 3

Horrible, Wonderful Sacrifice

PART I: PREPARATION

Bible passage: Genesis 22:1-19

Key verse: "God himself will provide the lamb for a burnt offering, my son" (Gen. 22:8).

Summary: God tells Abraham to sacrifice his son Isaac, who is the fulfillment of the promise to make Abraham a great nation. Abraham, who sometimes questions God, silently and willingly takes Isaac to the altar, binds him, and lays him on the pyre. Just as Abraham is about to kill Isaac, a ram appears in the briars nearby as a substitute sacrifice and Isaac is saved. The story has perplexed generations who cannot fathom how God could ask for the sacrifice of a child, especially the one who bears the promise of a whole nation. It is one thing for God to expect Abraham to believe in the promise. It is another thing for God to ask Abraham to be faithful when faith is costly. What happens to our faith when faith is costly as well as promising?

Study: The sacrifice of Isaac is a disturbing story. What are we to make of God asking a man to kill his son? What are we to think of Abraham, who skeptically questioned God in the last session, but who marches his own son to the altar of human sacrifice at God's command, no questions asked? What sense does it make for God to promise Abraham descendants and then take his only progeny? Christians have interpreted this story every which way over the centuries, struggling to find the meaning in it.

Bible scholar Walter Brueggemann cautions against trying to answer the vexing questions in Genesis 22. God is God. We cannot know all the reasons why something happens. But we get something else from this passage. We get a greater understanding of who God is and what faith is. The Abraham stories are not, he says, stories of the beginning of God's people; they are the stories of the beginning of faith.

Brueggemann points out some of the paradoxes about God in Genesis 22. Foremost is the clash between the side of God that tests people and demands absolute loyalty from them and the side that provides for the same people graciously and unconditionally. Abraham evidently displays the type of faith that grasps both at the same time. God tests. And in spite of what we may think about the all-knowing powers of God, it seems God does not know how this episode will turn out when the story begins. Only after Abraham raises his knife to kill Isaac and a ram appears in the briars as a substitute for Isaac does God finally say, "Now I know." Then in verse 16 God rewards Abraham because of how he chose to respond, not because he was predetermined to respond. If Abraham were "programmed" to respond always in faithfulness, God would not need to test, but Abraham is human and has a will of his own.

> Take my life, and let it be
> consecrated, Lord, to thee.
> Take my moments and my days;
> let them flow in ceaseless praise,
> let them flow in ceaseless praise.
>
> —Frances R. Havergal

Testing in the Bible

Testing is a theme in the stories of Abraham and elsewhere in the Bible. God's pattern is to first offer the promise with no conditions. God does not test Abraham first to see if he will be faithful. The first we see of Abraham, he is receiving an offer of a promise. Only later is Abraham's faith tested when God tells him to sacrifice his son and then waits to see if Abraham will do it. The same thing happens to Moses and the people Israel. Before they have a chance to prove themselves, God moves them toward the Promised Land, no strings attached. Then when they have escaped Egypt and are wandering in the wilderness, God tests their faith. Like Abraham, Israel questions whether the promise is real and whether they have done the right thing. Even Jesus is tested. His test comes in the desert when he is tempted and in the Garden of Gethsemane before his crucifixion.

Abraham knows God demands absolute loyalty. He also knows, by faith, that the ram in the bushes is a gift from God. He knows God is the source of life, in spite of the test. God takes away and God gives back, but these two actions are not logically connected.

The Promise

It's tempting to believe that since God has been revealed as a reliable promise keeper, Abraham would never really have been allowed to sacrifice his son. It's hard to imagine the end of the story any other way than the happy way it turned out. After all, why would God make a promise to Abraham that he would have many descendants and then take away the child who is the link to the nation of Israel? And isn't the end of the story foretold when Abraham says to the two attendants, "Stay here with the donkey; the boy and I will go over there; we will worship, and then we will come back to you" (22:5)?

And what about Abraham whom God has already pronounced righteous? Can't we be sure that Abraham is faithful and does not need to sacrifice Isaac? Again we are tempted to think that the story will come out well in the end. But remember chapter 21. Abraham had just sacrificed Ishmael, the original heir. At Sarah's command, Abraham banished Hagar and Ishmael to the desert where they would have surely died, had it not been for God's providence. We are often shocked at the thought of Abraham sacrificing Isaac and forget that he has already sacrificed his first born. Doesn't God know that Abraham is capable of deep sacrifice? Why does God need to test what is already known?

The rescue of Ishmael may lead us to yet another temptation, the temptation of thinking that God provides and would never let anything happen to Isaac. God is God. We cannot know what God will do. God provides, but God also allows the people to fail. At times in the biblical story, God allows the people to have their own way and live with the consequences. They are allowed to have a king like other people (1 Sam. 8). They are allowed to fail as a nation and be marched off to exile in Babylon. And they are allowed to sacrifice Jesus. Even God sacrifices a son. We cannot fully know God's ways.

The passage raises many questions, but it also gives powerful testimony to Abraham's faith and God's love. With tremendous faith Abraham is willing to give his most precious possession to God. He confidently relies on the God whom he has come to trust "will himself provide" (22:8). And God does provide. God provides water for the parched boy, Ishmael, in the desert and promises to make a nation for him, too. And God provides a ram at the right moment to replace Isaac on the altar. As the stories of the Bible build, it is the character of God that emerges, more so, perhaps, than the development of a nation. Out of these stories, we come to know who God is and who we are, or should be, as the people of God.

Things to think about: Talk with others this week about sacrifices they have made. Find out particularly if anyone in your community has "sacrificed" their children; that is, what decisions have parents made for faith that affected their children, such as choosing to be missionaries, taking a public stand on a controversial issue, picking a helping profession that took them away from family? How did these sacrifices turn out? Were they pleasing to God? to the children? Would people make the same sacrifices if they had it to do all over again?

PART II: SESSION

FOCUS (20 MINUTES)

Divide into three groups. Let one group represent families, one group represent country, and one group represent faith. Use the mind set of your group's designation to consider the situations below and decide if your group will sacrifice one of its members for the cause. Have one person in your group sit down for each situation in which your group would sacrifice a member.

- Rebels in a foreign country are fighting for democracy and your country decides to wade in on the side of the rebels. Will you send members of your group, knowing they may be sacrificed?
- An enemy nation overruns an island protectorate of your country. The government sends in the armed services. Will you send members of your group, knowing they may be sacrificed?
- Your ethnically homogeneous neighborhood is changing rapidly with the influx of other ethnic groups. At times neighbors get along well, but at other times tensions flare. Will you stay and perhaps sacrifice members of your family or the community to violence, or move to a safer place?
- Your sister community in a country cursed by civil war has asked you to send visitors to help lessen the violence. Are you willing to send people into this danger zone?
- A chemical reprocessing plant wants to locate a new facility in your community at a considerable economic gain to the community, but at some risk to public health. Would your group permit them to set up shop in your area?
- An AIDS hospice group wants to use the vacant parsonage next to your church for a hospice facility. Will you permit this to happen, even if members of your family and community may be exposed to the disease?

- A group of youth want to attend a work camp 1500 miles away. The most economical way of getting there is driving a van. Will you permit them to go, knowing there is potential for a serious accident?
- Your country has discovered a treatment for meningitis and wants to vaccinate all children, though there is a slight chance that a number of children will contract the disease from the vaccine and actually die from it. Will you vaccinate your children to stop the spread of the disease, even if your children could suffer or die?

When you have considered each situation, compare the number of people you have left standing with the number of people standing in the other two groups. What do the numbers say about the group's willingness to make sacrifices? For which type of thing will you make sacrifices? Country? Family? Faith? If one group has fewer standing than the other groups, why? If all groups have about the same number standing, why?

> Human sacrifice was not unheard of in the Ancient Near East. Perhaps the sacrifice of Isaac would not have affected other cultures of that region the way it affected Hebrew and Christian cultures. To name two, Assyrian and Canaanite religions practiced the rite of child sacrifice by burning.

Transition: Often we're willing to make costly sacrifices if we believe the cause is right and essential. Abraham finds out how costly faith is when God asks him to sacrifice his son Isaac. Dig into the story together to understand why God would ask for deep sacrifices and what they mean for your life.

Engage the Text (15 MINUTES)

This text (Gen. 22:1-19) has inspired many writers to speculate over Abraham's dilemma. Could any of us even consider killing a child, and could God ever ask us to do such a thing? Søren Kierkegaard, a Christian writer in the 1800s, asked these kinds of questions. This reader's theatre is loosely based on his thoughts.

Assign five people to be readers. If your group is small, assign more than one part per person. It may feel more alive if all the readers stand for the reading.

Reader's Theatre
1 - Then God called Abraham,
2 - "Abraham!"
3 - "Here I am," said Abraham.
2 - "Take your son Isaac, whom you love, and go to the land of Moriah,

and offer him there as a burnt offering on one of the mountains that I shall show you."

4 - Abraham did not talk to Sarah,

5 - and he did not tell his son Isaac what God had commanded.

4 - How could he explain it?

1 - Early in the morning, Abraham rose and prepared his donkey. Sarah kissed her son, Isaac, the son who was a miracle from God. The son whom she had carried for nine months. Abraham took two servants, his son, and wood for the sacrifice, and set out in the way God had shown him. Sarah watched them as they left. They traveled for three days, and on the third day Abraham looked up and saw the place that God had led him to.

3 - "Servants, stay here with the donkey. The boy and I will go over there,

4 - we will worship,

3 - and then we will come back to you."

1 - Abraham had Isaac carry the wood. Abraham carried the fire and the knife. Together they walked up the mountain.

2 - "Father!"

3 - "Here I am, my son," said Abraham.

2 - "The fire and the wood are here, but where is the lamb for the sacrifice?"

5 - Abraham did not say anything for a long time.

4 - He thought, "I could tell him what I am about to do,

5 - but will he believe me?

4 - Or will he think that God hates him? With his dying breath, will Isaac pray for another god to save him?

3 - Finally Abraham said, "God will provide, my son."

1 - Abraham felt a deep sadness.

4 - He dreaded the top of the mountain. He thought, Should I grab Isaac and tell him that this sacrifice is my own evil desire? Shall I tell him that his father has the power of life and death over his children? Then will I tell Isaac to pray to God, because God is his only hope? At least Isaac will not doubt the God I trust.

5 - Or will I grab my son and say nothing, leaving it for Isaac to wonder what is happening—

4 - as I wonder what is happening?

1 - They walked on together. When they had come to the place God had shown them, Abraham built an altar and laid the wood on it.

1 - He bound his son,

5 - laid him on the altar

1 - on top of the wood.

5 - Abraham reached out his hand...

4 - A terrible thought raced through Abraham's mind. What if I have failed? God, forgive my arrogance. How could I have known what

you wanted? I bound your precious child and raised my knife over him. Have I forgotten what it is to be a father? Have I defiled the promise you made to me?

1 - Abraham reached out his hand

5 - and took his knife

1 - to kill his son.

2 - Then an angel of God said, "Abraham! Abraham!"

3 - "Here I am."

2 - "Do not hurt the boy, for I now know that you fear God. You have not withheld your son, your only son, from me."

5 - Abraham looked around and saw a ram in the bushes. He cut Isaac's ropes.

4 - To himself, he whispered in relief, "Today God has given me a son."

1 - He took the ram and offered it as a burnt offering in the place of his son.

3 - Abraham said, "I will call this place 'The LORD will provide,' because on the mount of God, it will be provided."

2 - The angel of the LORD said, "Because you have not withheld your only son from me, I will indeed bless you and I will make your offspring as numerous as the stars in heaven and as sand on the seashore."

5 - Abraham returned to his servants. The servants did not ask their master about the groans they had heard.

1 - They did not ask their master why he said nothing to them.

5 - They did not ask their master's son why he was still shaking.

1 - In silence, they walked home.

Take some time to talk about the characters in this story. For each character—Abraham, God, Isaac, Sarah, and the servants—ask, *How do you think they felt before the episode on the mountain and after the episode on the mountain?*

Respond (10 MINUTES)

Take a piece of ribbon or yarn that has been prepared for each member of the group. Talk together about the following questions:

• Why would God ask a parent to sacrifice his or her child?
• When has God asked others, besides Abraham, to sacrifice a life?
• Is faith worth it if it means sacrificing members of the family?
• For what other reasons do we "sacrifice" family members?
• What have you felt God has asked you to do in order to demonstrate your trust in God?
• How does God's call to you affect other people around you?
• What is God calling you to do at the present time?

As the group responds to the final question, tie your ribbon or yarn somewhere on your person or possession (tie it on a finger, belt loop, purse). Let this ribbon be a symbol to you of both the promise and the cost of faith.

Closing (5 MINUTES)

In silent prayer, call out the names of heroes of the church who have made costly sacrifices, even their lives, for faith. Sing or read the words of the hymn "Take my life."

PART III: LEADER GUIDELINES

Items Needed

Bibles (to cross-reference the text as needed)
Small pieces of ribbon or yarn, enough for each member in the group

Resources

Anderson, Bernhard W. *Understanding the Old Testament.* Paramus, NJ: Prentice-Hall, 1986.
Kaiser, Walter C., Jr. *Hard Sayings of the Old Testament.* Downers Grove, Ill.: InterVarsity Press, 1988.

Tips for Leading

1. Make four-inch lengths of ribbon (1/4" or 1/2" wide) or yarn for each participant.
2. For greater effect, tap five people ahead of time to perform the readers theater and rehearse once before the session.
3. If you have a small group, give each subgroup in Focus ten index cards or slips of paper to represent people. Let the slips of paper represent the number of people they would sacrifice to causes.

Session 4
In the Name of Faith

■

PART I: PREPARATION

Bible passage: Genesis 12:10-20 and 13:1-18

Key verse: "Say you are my sister, so that it may go well with me because of you, and that my life may be spared on your account" (Gen. 12:13).

Summary: The story of Abraham's deception regarding Sarah and the story of Abraham dividing the land with Lot are two very different faith stories that, when taken together, form a whole. In the first, Abraham uses his own plan to thwart a threat to God's promise. In the second, Abraham faces another threat to the promise but leaves everything to God. Which way should it be? How should it be for us? Should we leave everything to God, or are there times we should take initiative to guard the promise?

Study: When God makes a promise of land and descendants for Abraham in chapter 12, Abraham's family uproots itself and goes, seemingly without question. But in verse 10 a famine comes over the land, forcing Abraham to migrate to Egypt and live as an alien. On their way to Egypt, Abraham tells Sarah to lie about being his wife. He worries that the Egyptians will see her beauty and her wealth and try to get to it by killing him. But if she is merely a sister, having her will not entitle anyone to Abraham's wealth. To protect everything that God has given them and promised them, Abraham tells Sarah to pose as his sister.

Perhaps the forced side trip and the dried up land shakes Abraham's confidence in God's promise. Or perhaps he feels overconfident about his role in making the promise happen. Or perhaps he honestly feels his partnership with God in the promise allows him to take things into his own hands. Like Adam and Eve's deception in the garden, Abraham seems to have his reasons. We can imagine him thinking that his own life is well worth the small charade. It's not appropriate to question his trust in the promise. We can only reason how Abraham might be thinking the promise will be fulfilled.

God intervenes when the story takes a turn that puts Sarah in the house of Pharaoh, perhaps as a wife. As the poet Sir Walter Scott notes, "Oh what tangled webs we weave, when first we practice to deceive." The situation is getting out of hand. God rescues Sarah, and Abraham for that matter, by sending plagues on Pharaoh and his household until Pharaoh begs the Hebrews to go away (see also Exod. 12:29-33). We don't know if God jumps into the fray out of anger, irritation, or concern. The text doesn't say. All we know is that God saves Abraham and saves the promise.

> Oh, what tangled webs we weave, when first we practice to deceive!
>
> —Sir Walter Scott

In chapter 13, we return to the Abraham we first knew, the Abraham who leaves everything to God. Abraham's entourage has done well, camped between Bethel and Ai, so well that they are bursting at the seams with people and livestock. At times, tempers of the overcrowded shepherds flare; conflict plagues them, not to mention that other peoples living in the area are competing for the same grasslands to feed their animals.

Abraham's solution is to spread out, giving Lot enough land for his people and his herds. Abraham doesn't map out the land that God has given him and give Lot the leftovers. He gives Lot first choice. Abraham trusts that God is in control and will give him the land that is his, so he is not worried about letting Lot take first pick of parcels. And, as we have seen with the other stories of promise and faith, Lot chooses the land that contains Sodom (an indication that this is not the Promised Land), and Abraham is left with Canaan, which we know in hindsight is the Promised Land.

God also comes to Abraham in defense of the promise in this story. After Lot has chosen the plains, God speaks to Abraham, offering him all the land in Canaan that he can see in each direction, a typical method for claiming land in the Ancient Near East. Whether or not Abraham has a part in fulfilling the promise, his faith in it is strong and God's intention of delivering it is steadfast. That the story of Abraham's deception and the story of parceling out the land appear in sequence tells us that Abraham is both human and still faithful, a good sign for us. But ultimately the placement of these stories tells us that it is God who is faithful.

Abraham and Sarah were clearly chosen by God to be the parents of God's people. Yet, Abraham's actions remind us several times that he and his family are human. Right off he concocts the deception about Sarah. He also bends to Sarah's pressure to send his beloved Ishmael and Hagar to die in the desert (21:8-14). We know that the story of the sacrifice of Isaac (22:1-14) is a story of faith, but we wonder whether Abraham isn't making a mistake, that perhaps his faith has gone awry. These stories only serve to show how human Abraham and Sarah really are.

She's My Sister

When Abraham and Sarah go to Egypt, Abraham lies about his wife, saying that she is his sister. Abraham has his own rationale for lying. For one, the threat of losing his wife was real. Rulers such as Pharaoh typically took many wives. For another, the story of King David taking Bathsheba for a wife and having her husband killed shows that God's people were not above wife stealing and that Abraham's life may actually be in danger.

Moreover, Abraham may be trying to solve the problem of not having an heir. (The riches he received from Pharaoh when Sarah was taken into the court allowed Abraham to obtain a new wife. Such a thing was culturally acceptable, and God had not yet definitively said that the heir would be from Sarah. In fact, Abraham later produces an heir with Hagar. Besides, Abraham's deception is not great. Genesis 20:12 suggests, in fact, that Sarah is already Abraham's half-sister. Nevertheless, he lets Sarah be taken as Pharaoh's wife to save his own skin and increase his wealth.

God curses Pharaoh for what he did, though Pharaoh could not have known better. He may have thought his family would also be blessed by Abraham. Recall that in Genesis 12:1-3 God says all the families of the earth would be blessed and cursed through Abraham. Rather than a blessing, however, Abraham's deceit causes a curse to Pharaoh. And even though it is Abraham who is deceitful, God's favour stays with him.

A Different Way

Genesis 13 also puts the promise in the context of family. This time it's Abraham and his nephew Lot. Lot chooses one way, the way of the fertile plains, but the land also contains the city of Sodom. Abraham does not choose. He simply believes. He believes that the promise will be fulfilled. The promise is not something that we choose or don't choose. It simply is. We choose whether or not to believe it or accept it, and then we live with the consequences. Lot's fate grows out of his lack of belief. But in this case Abraham gets it right.

Things to think about: Take a poll this week at work or among friends. Ask a number of people if it is okay to lie if lying will help you or someone else, such as lying to an enemy. And will lying get you in trouble with God? Bring the results of your poll to the group meeting.

PART II: SESSION

FOCUS (10 MINUTES)

Option A: With a pencil or pen, answer each of the following questions with one of these responses: always, never, or sometimes.

1. If a bank teller accidentally gave you an extra $20 bill, would you give it back?
2. If you were a parent and discovered a pack of cigarettes in your daughter's coat pocket, would you talk to her about it?
3. If you were a college student, would you save money by photocopying a required textbook?
4. If you were a plumber on a vacation with your family and the hotel you were staying in needed emergency help, would offer your services?
5. If you had your own business, would you use your expense account to mix business and pleasure?
6. If you opened the door of your truck and dented the car beside you, would you leave a note?
7. If you were a parent of a 15-year-old boy and discovered a condom in his pocket as you were washing his jeans, would you talk to him about it?
8. If you were selling a good-looking car with worn brakes and an almost broken engine, would you tell prospective buyers about the problems if they didn't ask?
9. If your friend lets you borrow a CD, would you record a copy of it for yourself?
10. If you had deep questions about your faith and stopped going to church regularly, would you answer honestly if a pastor asked you why?

Ask, *What question was the hardest for you to answer? Why? In that case, what would likely happen if you took another course of action?*

Option B: Make up your own "everyday dilemmas." Tell a partner about a situation you faced when you had to make an ethical decision between two equal options. Ask your partner what he or she would have done.

Compare your decision with your partner's response. Then listen to your partner's dilemma and tell what you would have done.

Transition: Since time immemorial we humans have faced tough decisions. Even Abraham, the man God chose to fulfill the promise, faced tough situations. And he took more than one approach to solving them. Let's see what he did.

Engage the Text (15 MINUTES)

Divide into two groups. Group 1 will study the Abraham and Sarah story. Group 2 will study the Abraham and Lot story. Quickly jot down answers to these questions.

1. Where are the people headed at the beginning of the story?
2. What threat to the promise do they face?
3. How does Abraham address the threat?
4. What does God do?
5. What happens in the end?

Come back together as a whole group and compare answers to see where the stories are parallel and where they differ. What did you find?

Go back to your small group and take only a couple of minutes with your group to rewrite the ending of the story. Tell how the story would have ended if Abraham had been honest in the first place and dishonest in the second. In what way would God's response have been different, if at all? Come back together and retell the story with the new ending.

> If they manage to carry out their threats, I shall be offering my blood for the redemption and resurrection of El Salvador. Martyrdom is a grace from God that I do not believe I have earned. But if God accepts the sacrifice of my life, then may my blood be the seed of liberty, and a sign of the hope that will soon become a reality.
>
> —Archbishop Oscar Romero

Respond (15 MINUTES)

Talk briefly as a group about God's promise to our generation. What do you think God has promised us through the ministry, life, death, and resurrection of Jesus?

Then arrange yourselves on an imaginary spectrum with one end representing Faith and the other end representing Action. If you believe that God requires you to have faith, but no responsibility for fulfilling the promise, stand at the Faith end. If you believe that you must live and act a certain way for the promise to be fulfilled, stand at the Action end. If you believe that both are true to some extent stand in the middle. You may find that you lean more heavily one way than the other.

Take turns telling why you are standing where you are. Also, tell how God may have intervened in situations of either type, Faith or Action. Or, in other words, is God ultimately in control? Why or why not?

Closing (5 MINUTES)

One: Go in love,
All: for love alone endures.
One: Go in peace,
All: for it is the gift of God.
One: Go in safety,
All: for we cannot go where God is not.

By Earle W. Fike, Jr. Used by permission of Brethren Press.

PART III: LEADER GUIDELINES

Items Needed

Bibles
Bible atlas, commentary, and concordance
Paper and pens

Tips for Leading

1. Have on hand Bibles, pens, paper, a Bible atlas, a commentary, and a concordance. These may be helpful when you study the Bible text.
2. If members of the group are reticent to speak, try using newsprint and markers to write down responses. Sometimes a list of things will trigger a response in others.
3. Be prepared with examples from your own life to get the conversation going in each section of the session. If others are ready to speak at first, hold your comments for later.
4. If your group is not inclined to move around or work in small groups, use the suggestions above as questions for the whole group. Tailor the activities for the needs of your group.

Looking ahead: Be prepared ahead of time for Option A in

Respond. Find out what controversies are stirring in your community. Offer them for the exercise if the group is unsure about local conflicts.

Session 5

How Many Virtuous People Does It Take to...

PART I: PREPARATION

Bible passage: Genesis 18:16–19:29

Key verse: Then Abraham came near and said [to God], ". . . Suppose there are fifty righteous within the city; will you then sweep away the place and not forgive it for the fifty righteous who are in it? Far be it from you to do such a thing" (Gen. 18:23-25).

Summary: Abraham is visited by God and two angels. Together they set off toward Sodom, discussing God's plan to annihilate the city. Abraham wants to know whether God would actually destroy righteous people living in Sodom along with sinners. Or if the righteous can save the wicked, how many righteous people would it take to save them? When God does finally destroy Sodom, it is the righteousness of one man, Abraham, that saves Lot and his family. The fact that the city was destroyed leads us to ask today how more of us could be righteous in order to save the wicked of the world. And the fact that God dealt compassionately with Lot leads us to ask ourselves how our God is different from the gods who predictably dole out punishments for sins and rewards for righteousness.

Study: The story of Sodom and Gomorrah has become synonymous in our thinking with sin and depravity. The destruction of the cities is the quintessential example of what will happen to us if we're not good. But set in the scope of Genesis, the significance of these stories is almost opposite of what we usually think. Genesis 18 and 19 are stories of how the righteous can help the wicked and how God is compassionate even for the wicked.

The passage consists of two main parts. The first, Genesis 18:16-33, is a dialogue between God and Abraham. Here Abraham and God switch roles. Abraham becomes the teacher and God the listening student. We have seen Abraham engage God in honest dialogue before. This time, it's almost more than honest, it's brazen. Walter Brueggemann notes that a very early copy of this Bible text says that "God stood before Abraham" but that ancient scribes may have been uncomfortable with the image of God subordinated to a human. So the text says "Let me take it upon myself to speak to the Lord, I who am but dust and ashes" (v. 27) addressing the "Judge of all the earth" (v. 25).

> Will you indeed sweep away the righteous with the wicked? Suppose there are fifty righteous within the city; will you then sweep away the place and not forgive it for the fifty righteous who are in it? Far be it from you to do such a thing, to slay the righteous with the wicked, so that the righteous fare as the wicked!
>
> —Genesis 18:23-25

Their discussion (or Abraham's lecture!) puts the whole idea of judgment in an entirely new light. Isn't it God's role to judge and punish sin? No doubt it is. But Abraham's God, whom we are getting to know in these stories, does not judge according to any formula, at least not the one we expect. This God takes into account the fact that there is righteousness mixed in with wickedness and that to destroy one is to destroy the other. God also remembers the promise made to Abraham despite the weaknesses of the people. To destroy all evil would be to destroy all possibility of fulfilling the promise.

Notice that God's judgment on Sodom and Gomorrah is set up almost like a lawyer questioning a witness. Legal language such as this is frequently used in the Bible for judging. In the story of Noah and the flood, for example, the nature of crime is announced along with a consequence (Gen. 6:11-13). This legal form is highly developed in the first few chapters of Amos. Amos proclaims that "for three transgressions of Damascus, and for four, [the LORD] will not revoke the punishment; because they have threshed Gilead. . . [therefore] I will send a fire . . ." (Amos 1:3-4). While in Genesis the language is legalese, the message is one of grace. God finally says to Abraham that it takes only a little bit of righteousness to make up for a wealth of wickedness.

An "Outcry"

In Genesis 18:20 God tells Abraham about a complaint against Sodom and Gomorrah. There has been an "outcry" against those cities. *Outcry* is a legal term in the Bible for the way oppressed people call out for justice. We're not certain why God wants to talk with Abraham about the situation, except that the two have a relationship now. This God does not always act unilaterally, but consults with Abraham. And Abraham does not always acquiesce, but questions and confides honestly in God. Here Abraham intervenes with a petition for God to show mercy.

The legal language shows that God can judge and mete out punishment. God can give people what they deserve. And, unfortunately, bad people might take good people with them. This is the image that the gods of neighbouring peoples might have had. But in spite of God's power to behave this way, God does something different. God hears the pleas of people. God wants to find a way to save.

Communal Guilt

In the second part of this passage (Gen. 19:1-29), God, in fact, decides to condemn both cities for the sins of the wicked. In contrast to the way our legal system judges the guilt of individuals, the culture in Abraham's time often saw guilt as a condition of the whole community. Whole families, their descendants, or even a home town might have received punishment for the actions of one person. Though it's worth noting, as does Eugene Roop in his book *Genesis,* the actions of a few in our own culture have consequences for many when it comes to nuclear weapons or environmental destruction.

Just as the community bears responsibility for one person's sin, so does it benefit from the virtue of a few. God puts responsibility on humans to be righteous in order to save the wicked. Lot is saved because he is righteous. He was hospitable to the angels who came to warn him, and hospitality is an important righteous act in the Bible. But Lot is also hesitant, lingering in his house and refusing to leave (19:15-23). It is more likely that it is was Abraham's virtue that saved Lot. "So it was that, when God destroyed the cities of the Plain, God remembered Abraham, and sent Lot out of the midst of the overthrow, when he overthrew the cities in which Lot had settled" (19:29). Apparently it takes only one righteous man to save others. As followers of Jesus, we know this to be true. What was Abraham thinking as he looked out over the destruction? Perhaps he looked back at his "courtroom" debate with God and wondered what would have not happened if God had been more compassionate, but if the people had been more righteous.

Hospitality

The sin of Sodom is a hotly debated topic. Whatever it is, it is probably the opposite of hospitality. In the culture of the Ancient Near East, offering hospitality to visitors was a high priority and an honour. Here the theme of hospitality begins even before the story of Sodom and Gomorrah. It starts when Abraham and Sarah welcome the three visitors in Genesis 18:1-15. Then Abraham journeys with them toward Sodom, where finally the two angels stay in Lot's house. The rabble outside the house, who want to abuse the visitors, represent the opposite of hospitality.

Lot's offer of his daughters to the mob is a difficult passage. It has often been suggested that while we, and the Israelites, find it abhorrent, it is meant to symbolically show the lengths to which Lot would go to protect his guests. Gerald Janzen has suggested in his book on Abraham that Lot's offer was rhetorical—the unexpected offer of his virgin daughters was intended to shock the mob and make them realize their immorality.

Similarly, the text is not implying that the number of righteous people needed to save the city is literally ten. The story illustrates that God is not a rigid scorekeeper. Rather, it is symbolic of the small amount of righteousness it takes to save.

Which is more important, righteousness or wickedness, when God judges an injustice? If it is wickedness, then the many deserve the punishment of the few. But God reveals in the end that God pays more attention to righteousness, and the good of a few can save the many.

Things to think about: This week talk with others to compare the use of righteousness and wickedness in the legal system and in a family system. Which is the basis of the legal system? Which is the basis of family systems? What would happen if these were switched?

To prepare for this session, think of situations around you, or elsewhere in your community or the world, that are seemingly hopeless. As you read the newspaper or listen to the news, clip out stories or jot them down. Bring these situations to the group and offer them as prayer concerns in the latter half of the session.

PART II: SESSION

Focus (10 MINUTES)

Option A: Do an improvisational exercise. Find a partner. Look over the following words: *discussion, debate, bargain, argument, fight.* Stand facing your partner, ready to formulate a "discussion" about a controversial topic that members of the rest of the group will suggest, such as Fords are better than Chevies, TV is okay for you, or evolution is bunk. Improvise a "discussion" on the controversial topic for about two minutes. Stop the action. Then improvise a "debate." Try a new controversy or keep the same one as before. Repeat for all five words.

Option B: As a group, arrange the five words above according to their levels of emotional intensity. Then suggest examples of when discussion is the most appropriate form of communication. When is a debate the most appropriate form of communication? List examples for the remaining three words as well.

Transition: When two people bargain with each other, it's a two-way interaction. Both put forth suggestions, and both listen to the other's response. It's refreshing to think that our relationship with God can be like this. God is a living being that is open to our concerns, questions, and requests. Abraham demonstrates this as he stands talking with God outside the city of Sodom. Let's take a closer look at this story in Genesis.

> According to [Jewish tradition], the world reposes upon thirty-six Just Men, the Lamed-Vov, indistinguishable from simple mortals; often they are unaware of their station. But if just one of them were lacking, the sufferings of mankind would poison even the souls of the newborn, and humanity would suffocate with a single cry. For the Lamed-Vov are the hearts of the world multiplied, and into them, as into one receptacle, pour all our griefs...."And it is known that some remain forever inconsolable at human woe, so that God himself cannot warm them. So from time to time the Creator, blessed be His Name, sets forward the clock of the Last Judgment by one minute."
>
> —André Schwarz-Bart, *The Last of the Just*

Engage the Text (15 MINUTES)

Listen to a reader read Genesis 18:16–19:29 out loud. Then divide into two groups. With Bibles in hand, Group 1 will retell the story using only the verses that emphasize God as judge. Group 2 will do the same, except they will use only the verses that emphasize God's compassion. Read the edited versions of the story to each other.

Talk together about which view of God is the "right" view. Why? To what extent are both true?

Respond (15 MINUTES)

Option A: As a group, list some of the human problems in your church or community that are potentially divisive or destructive. Choose one to work on. As a group, devise two strategies for addressing the problem. Approach the problem once with the aim of getting rid of the "culprits." Approach it again with the aim of changing the situation through the strengths or virtues of the community. For instance, you might be dealing with drug problems. Simplistically speaking, one approach is to use the law to cut off supply. The other approach is to provide drug education to youth to try to decrease demand.

Compare the effectiveness and faithfulness of both approaches. Also discuss whether the community and the church can be expected to operate from the same set of values when it comes to social problems. How about when dealing with religious problems?

Option B: Talk briefly about the extent of your responsibility to be righteous on behalf of others. How can your personal righteousness make a difference for others? Where have you seen many people suffer for the sins of a few? Where have you seen others benefit from the righteousness of one or more people?

Arrange your chairs in a circle. In a time of prayer, focus on some of the situations you have read about in the paper or seen on the news. Remember that God hears our prayers. As Abraham demonstrated, the faith of a few can make a difference to God.

As you pray, share with God your concerns for peace, justice, mercy, and compassion. If you feel led, voice your frustrations as well. Identify the needs you see and ask for mercy. Argue with God, if you feel comfortable. The prayer is over when everyone who wants to has had an opportunity to share.

Closing (10 MINUTES)

Stand in a circle and join hands. Tell how the person to your left is righteous and will "save" others. When you are finished, squeeze the hand of the person on your left as an indication you are finished and he or she may begin.

PART III: LEADER GUIDELINES

Items Needed

Bibles
Chalkboard and chalk or newsprint and markers

Resources

Roop, Eugene F. *Genesis* (Believers Church Bible Commentary).
  Scottdale: Herald Press, 1987.

Tips for Leading

1. Moderate the Focus activity, making sure the improvisations don't carry
   on too long. If you have a large group, have all pairs do the exercise at
   the same time. Allow no more than two minutes for each style of communication. Call time at the end of the limit and move on to the next
   one. The more quickly this exercise goes, the more useful it will be.
2. Try the Engage the Text exercise yourself sometime before the session
   begins. If a group falters, you can step in to give them ideas and a
   starting point.
3. In Respond, judge whether your group is more inclined to discuss or
   pray and meditate. All groups have character. One style of activity may
   be more meaningful than another.

Looking ahead: Bring a copy of the church budget to session 6. A
budget showing income *and* assets would be the most useful.

Plan time in the session next week to evaluate this study of Abraham.
Talk about what people liked and didn't like, what they learned, and how
they might have changed.

Session 6
Playing
Favourites

PART I: PREPARATION

Bible passage: Genesis 21:8-21; 25:21-34

Key verse: Abraham rose early in the morning, and took bread and a skin of water, and gave it to Hagar, putting it on her shoulder, along with the child [Ishmael], and sent her away. And she departed, and wandered about in the wilderness of Beer-sheba. (Gen. 21:14)

Summary: Abraham and Sarah favoured their son Isaac over Abraham's son Ishmael. After Abraham died and Isaac had children of his own, he too picked a favourite—Esau over Jacob. But his wife Rebekah favoured Jacob. It's not uncommon for parents to sometimes favour one child over another, but does that mean a parent loves one child over another? Does our parent, God, play favourites among the children of God? Or for that matter, how does God regard children of other faiths?

Study: Election is a central concept in the Old Testament. To be "elected" by God means to be chosen. God chooses a people to whom to relate and makes a promise to them. They belong to God in a special way. In the Old Testament, the people of Israel understand their relationship to God in this way. They are "set apart" from other nations. They have had a special relationship with God, and God expects them to live and act in a special way.

The reason for this favouritism is not Israel's number or might, or even their faithfulness. Rather, God loves the people and faithfully keeps the promises made to them. Elsewhere, it is written that because Israel received God's favour, Israel ought to treat those from other nations and the weak in its own society in a favourable way (Deut. 10:17-19). They are to love and treat justly the stranger and the traveler in their midst.

God's love turns out to be all-encompassing. Those outside the special group also fall under God's care. Genesis scholar Walter Brueggemann distinguishes between God's love for the chosen or elected and God's love for those who are not chosen, but treasured nonetheless, like Ishmael. Ishmael also receives a promise, though it is a lesser one. He will be the father of a nation, but not God's chosen people. God will be with him, demonstrating that divine love extends to those who are "treasured" but not elected.

> If a man has two wives, one of them loved and the other disliked, and if both the loved and the disliked have borne him sons, the firstborn being the son of the one who is disliked, then on the day when he willed his possessions to his sons, he is not permitted to treat the son of the loved as the first-born in preference to the son of the disliked, who is the firstborn. He must acknowledge as firstborn the son of the one who is disliked, giving him a double portion of all that he has; since he is the first issue of his virility, the right of the firstborn is his.
>
> —Deuteronomy 21:15-17

Hard to Take

The favouritism shown to some but not to others in the Abraham stories is likely troubling to our way of thinking, especially when it crosses the lines of insiders and outsiders. In the biblical stories, there is much ambiguity about God's favouritism. Isaac, Sarah, and Jacob are favoured. Ishmael, Hagar, and Esau (one of the chosen) are not, even though they are treasured.

Ishmael is Abraham's oldest son. He was conceived to be Abraham's heir and Hagar may rightly have felt that a decent inheritance was owed to him. Nevertheless, God tells Abraham and Sarah that Isaac is to be the heir to God's promises. Like the other favourites in the Bible, Isaac was born of "nothing." His mother was barren, unlike Ishmael's mother.

It is a theme in Genesis that the beginning of the world and the beginning of faith come from nothing. The world is created from a void. A flood decimates the earth and Noah starts over again from nothing. Sarah is old and barren, yet from her comes the fulfillment of the promise and the beginning of faith. Rebekah also is barren, yet she produces Jacob and Esau. Those who come from nothing to fulfill the promise are the favored ones.

Something from Nothing

Sarah, the barren one, and Hagar, the fertile one, come into conflict over the favour of Abraham, and ultimately God's favor. It may even seem that Sarah acts worse than Hagar. As a foreign slave-woman, Hagar is a real outsider. It was a coup in the first place for her to have had the opportunity to mother an heir. But Sarah sends Hagar away, presumably to her death. In 21:12, God even tells Abraham to go along with Sarah's banishment of Hagar, because Sarah has been chosen to mother the heir. In that moment, Abraham's concern extends to Ishmael, his flesh and blood, but not to Ishmael's mother.

> But what does the scripture say? "Drive out the slave and her child; for the child of the slave will not share the inheritance with the child of the free woman." So then, friends, we are children, not of the slave but of the free woman.
>
> —Galatians 4:30-31

Yet God does provide for Hagar. God is revealed to Hagar in the desert, and Hagar gives a name to God in 16:13— *El-roi*, meaning "God hears." We will see the God "who hears" again in the story of the Exodus. But even now, God's love extends beyond the immediately chosen and favoured family; but this love is different from that shown to Sarah. Sarah is the first in a long line of barren or unlikely women through whom the promise of heirs are fulfilled, including Rebekah, Rachael, Ruth, and Mary, mother of Jesus. Hagar cannot be counted among them.

Upsetting the Natural Order

By the time we get to the story of Jacob and Esau (Gen. 25:21-34), the pattern of favouritism is already established, but there is a new twist. Esau expects to be the favoured son. After all, he is the older, or the firstborn of the twins at least, and Isaac favours him over Jacob. However, God proclaims a reversal before the birth ever happens. There is no justification given, just an announcement that the older shall serve the younger (25:23). God chooses to upset what people understand to be the natural order of things.

Just as the theme of "something from nothing" goes against the natural order of things, so do the stories of inheritance in the Bible. It is the one who by rights should easily have the inheritance that usually loses. David, the youngest of twelve children, inherits the throne (1 Sam. 16) instead of his oldest brother. The younger son in Luke 15 (commonly known as the Prodigal Son) receives his inheritance ahead of his older brother.

In this story, Esau, the firstborn, takes his birthright lightly and trades it away to Jacob. For his part, Jacob, whose name means "he grabs by the heel," grabs for Esau's status as oldest son. While Jacob appears to be an opportunist in this story, he is the shepherd who knows how to multiply the herd and shows the most promise in creating heirs, metaphorically and in reality. When he is grown, Jacob marries Rachel, a barren woman (30:1), but as usual in the Bible, something comes from nothing again and their union eventually produces Joseph, the favoured of Jacob's twelve sons. The order of things in God's universe is not the order of things as we think it should be. God is full of surprises.

A Plague of Conflict

As in all families, conflict arises in God's family when things get out of their "natural" order. Esau becomes bitter toward Jacob for having tricked him out of his birthright. But just as God treasured Ishmael and gave him land of his own, God treasures Esau anyway, blessing him with the land of Edom.

Though the brothers are reconciled in this way, the Bible tells that the descendants of Jacob frequently fought with Esau's descendants, the nation of Edom. Under King David, Israel (Jacob) actually defeated Edom. The good news of the family is, however, that whatever the brothers and their descendants feel toward each other, they are God's possessions, heirs of the promise of the God who hears, the God who blesses, and the God who saves.

The Sons of Ishmael in Genesis 25 are possibly the twelve heads of the tribes of Ishmael, who make up the nation God promised to Abraham's firstborn and his mother, Hagar. Arab Muslims consider Ishmael the patriarch of their faith and the heir of a promise. Like Jacob's twelve sons, Ishmael's sons make up twelve Arab tribes.

Things to think about: Look at old family photos this week. How did your parents love each child in your family differently? How do you love each child in your immediate or extended family according to their needs? What rivalries did you and your siblings have? What rivalries do your children have?

PART II: SESSION

Focus (15 MINUTES)

Work as a group to dole out an imaginary inheritance to the youth in your congregation or to the families of group members. If your group is large, break into smaller groups of no more than six to make out "the will." Quickly decide what your assets are as a church or group (bank accounts, property, real estate, investments), and decide who should get what and why.

Reflect on how you made your decisions. To what extent did you try to be equal? To what extent did you consider how much each youth was deserving? What criteria did you use to decide who was most deserving?

Transition: We find ourselves in a quandary sometimes, trying to be fair and loving toward all our children, but knowing that some are favourites. We wonder if we should have those feelings? According to Genesis 12, God wants to be a blessing to all the nations of the world, but in the biblical story, God has favourites who get the full promise, while others get a lesser promise. Go to the stories of Isaac and Ishmael and Jacob and Esau in Genesis to see whom God favours and perhaps why.

Engage the Text (15 MINUTES)

Talk briefly about what troubles you about this passage, if anything. How does favouritism jive with what you know of God? What does God think not only about the less favorite within the faith but about people, like Ishmael, outside the faith?

Try modernizing the story. Sometimes stories in the ancient texts feel far removed from our present-day lives. We sometimes say, "Oh, it was different in those days." To bring the story of favour to life today, recast it with modern details.

Work in groups of two or three people to write a modern version of either the Isaac/Ishmael story or the Jacob/Esau story. Read the original story together first, then generate ideas for a new setting and characters for the story line. Spend no more than ten minutes rewriting the story.

Come back together to share your "new revised standard version" of the stories. Then talk about insights you gained, if any, by modernizing the story. Also talk about what still troubles you about the story.

Consider sharing your rewrites with the pastor or worship committee who could make use of them for dramas in worship.

Respond (15 MINUTES)

Option A: Look back at the study in Part I to see the distinction between the elect and the treasured. As a group, devise a list of people in your community who are "elect" (those who represent something from nothing, the most unlikely people who are actually heirs of the promise) and a list of treasured people (loved and valuable servants of God, but not elect). Which do you feel you are? Why? What could you do, if anything, to move from simply being treasured to being elect? What are the dangers of classifying church people this way? What's helpful about it?

Option B: In terms of nations, these stories from Genesis indicate that Israel is God's elect people, but God still treasures other nations. Talk about what this means for Christians sharing the world with people of other faiths. How should Christians regard people of other faiths? What does chosenness or election mean for you?

Closing (3 MINUTES)

Jacob and Esau were estranged for a long time by their rivalry, until finally they are reunited. Listen as someone reads the passage about their reconciliation.

> Now Jacob looked up and saw Esau coming, and four
> hundred men with him. So he divided the children
> among Leah and Rachel and the two maids....He him-
> self went on ahead of them, bowing himself to the
> ground seven times, until he came near his brother. But
> Esau ran to meet him, and embraced him, and fell on
> his neck and kissed him, and they wept. (Gen. 33:1-4)

Pray silently that all people—insiders and outsiders, elect and treasured, favoured and loved—can live together as God's people, people of the promise.

PART III: LEADER GUIDELINES

Items Needed

Bibles
Paper and pens or pencils

Tips for Leading

1. Ahead of time obtain a roster of the youth in the congregation for the Focus activity. In the exercise, steer people away from dwelling on any individual's weaknesses, focusing instead on the strengths of youth and their deservedness.
2. Before you begin Engage the Text, give people a chance to talk about their personal and theological understanding of the stories. These difficult passages are open to wide interpretation. Try to gauge how interested people are in sharing their views before you launch into the exercise modernizing the stories.

3. This is the final session on Abraham and his family. Consider making time to review the material from all six sessions. How do these sessions tie together as the story of the beginning of faith? What new insights have people gained? What difficult issues emerged that the group will continue to consider?